The Wild Elemental Oracle

Michelle Motuzas

REDFeather™
MIND | BODY | SPIRIT
4880 Lower Valley Road, Atglen, PA 19310

Library of Congress Control Number: 2020930559

Box design, cover, and layout by Danielle D. Farmer
Type set in Forplay/Minion Pro

ISBN: 978-0-7643-5989-7
Printed in China
7 6 5 4

Published by Red Feather Mind, Body, Spirit
An imprint of Schiffer Publishing, Ltd.
4880 Lower Valley Road
Atglen, PA 19310
Phone: (610) 593-1777; Fax: (610) 593-2002
E-mail: Info@schifferbooks.com
Web: www.redfeathermbs.com

"The clearest way into the Universe is through a Forest wilderness."

—John Muir

DEDICATION

ALEX AND GIAN
WHO ARE MY HEROES.

HEIDI
WHO HAS ALWAYS BELIEVED IN ME.

MY OWN CREATURES OF WISDOM
DANI & LUNA.

CONTENTS

EARTH

FIRE

WATER

AIR

INTRODUCTION

Man has been living alongside animals for millions of years. They have provided us with food, protection, and material for tools, shelter, and clothing. All indigenous people have had intimate relationships with the animals in their regions. Animals have served a variety of spiritual functions, and they have been linked with supernatural forces, acted as guardians and shamans, and appeared in images of an afterlife. They have even been worshipped as agents of gods and goddesses. Our ancestors honored the creatures that allowed them to live and flourish. They understood the innate wisdom of the forest, the jungle, the tundra, the sea, and the desert.

Much of this wisdom and co-dependence has been lost with the advent of industrialization, modern monolithic religions, and the departure from a tribal-based society and culture. We live very far removed from the animals that we as humans once co-evolved with. Our animal-based food is processed and packaged in styrofoam and cellophane and offered in huge fluorescent-lit grocery stores. Our leather clothing is ordered online or found in chic little boutiques. We decimate forests for wood for our housing without ever seeing the trees the material came from.

Thankfully there is a movement, both in and outside of a spiritual path, that is bringing people closer to the old ways.

However, most of us are not living in a society that is in day-to-day connection with the animals around us. We may visit animals at a zoo or animal sanctuary, but besides our pets and the random raccoon, squirrel, or other urban or suburban critter, daily animal contact is not a part of our lives anymore.

The Wild Elemental Oracle is a tool to be used to access the messages, wisdom, and lessons that the animal world brings us.

By no means is this an exhaustive list of the animals that bring us messages. I have used the context of working with the elements to divide the messages into categories.

The four basic elements are *Air*, *Earth*, *Fire*, and *Water*. Understanding what each element represents will help you evaluate where you need to focus your attention and energy for the situation you are asking about.

In a similar fashion, the Minor Arcana of the Tarot allows, at a glance, a reader to see a predominant aspect or theme in a reading. Are the majority of the cards water? It's an emotional issue. Fire? A situation that is connected to will, power, or creating.

The Elements

EARTH

(North and Feminine)

Earth represents grounding, the foundation of life, substance, connection to life path, family roots, nurturing, manifestation, abundance, dreams, and reality.

Earth can be fierce—such as with volcanoes and earthquakes.

WATER

(West and Feminine)

Water represents emotional release, intuition, inner reflection, intentions, love, devotion, happiness, thankfulness, compassion, physic development, community, healing relationships, ebb and flow, and mutability.

Water can be calm and soothing like the surface of a lake, or destructive and violent as in a torrential rain storm or a crashing surf.

FIRE

(South and Masculine)

Fire represents energy, a tool for transformation, connection to personal power, passion, compulsion, zeal, creativity, motivation, and determination.

Fire requires boundaries. Fire is combustible with air energy. Fire consumes but gives back light and warmth.

AIR

(East and Masculine)

Air represents intellect, mental intention, connection to universal life force, teacher, creation, first breath of life, wisdom, spirit, soul, and spiritual faith.

Air/wind cannot be controlled, but it can be harnessed.

ANIMAL GUIDES, ALLIES, & POWER ANIMALS

When animals come to us, it is under many different names: a totem, spirit guide, animal messenger, or teacher. It seems that there are as many different names as there are animals. Or are there?

For this book and deck I will use the term Spirit Animal to encompass the meaning of an animal spirit or messenger that has a message for you. This is an animal that joins you on your spiritual journey.

> **SPIRIT ANIMAL**
>
> *A teacher or messenger who comes in the form of an animal and has a personal relationship with you.*

Can I have more than one Spirit Animal?

YES!

Though your lifetime, it is my belief that you have one or two major Spirit Guides or totems. These stay with you your entire life. It is their job to be your teacher, offer protection, comfort, and assist with decisions, if you allow it. Always remember that we have free will. A true guide will never shame you, diminish you, be mean, or speak malevolently about anything.

Some people differentiate between animal spirits and more "human" forms of guides, such as an ancestor, ascended master, or angel. I do not. For those of us who resonate deeply with nature and the animal kingdom, our guides can come in the form of animals. For people with a more Christian leaning, they may see their guides as angels. Energy is pure energy. Our guides can and do take on any form that will resonate with each of us. We all have different backgrounds, religious beliefs, cultural constructs, and leanings that would make us more prone to accept a guide that shows up as an angel, or a bear, or an old Japanese man. If you have this deck, there is at least a part of you that resonates with the animal kingdom and the messages they bring!

No matter the form in which your guides show themselves to you, the core of this is energy. How the energy manifests is primarily driven by a persons belief system and the way they can accept and use the guidance and wisdom to the greatest good.

Throughout your journey in this life, and because of the ebb and flow of your life, situations and lessons, different spirit animals will come to you at different times to offer wisdom, direction, and strength.

You do not choose the animal; the animal chooses you. They provide guidance, lessons, protection, power, wisdom, and symbolism for you to use and draw on in all stages of your journey.

How do your Spirit Animals show up?

You may see an animal in person or one may show themselves to you over and over again in the form of photos, news articles, a stuffed animal that catches your attention in a store, or a combined synchronicity of many different ways. You may be visited in your dreams or during meditation. Trust that if this animal is meant to bring you messages you WILL notice it.

When an animal shows up, it typically represents qualities you need to look at in yourself. Pay attention to the animal's habitat.

- Are they nocturnal?
- What are their specific habits?
- What is their diet?
- How do they interact with their environment?
- Are they predator or prey?
- Do they act or react?
- Are they group oriented or loners?
- Are they active or sedentary?

Take a look at their strengths and their vulnerabilities. What about their nature speaks to where you are in your life right now? What situations can you apply their lessons or medicine to?

How do I know what my spirit animal is?

As mentioned before, I believe we have one or two main spiritual totems or guides throughout our lives. One whose message, identity, and path somehow closely align with the one you are on in this lifetime.

> If you are curious about your lifetime Spirit Animal guide, you can simply ask for it to be shown. This may take place in a dream or meditation, a journey or other visual manifestations; there are energy workers who can assist you if you feel unsure about your abilities. I will have a way for you to ask and get answers with this deck.

HOW DO YOU CONDUCT A READING FOR YOURSELF AND OTHERS?

Card readings, whether for yourself or others, are an individual process. It can take a lifetime of practice to master your own intuitive system. Fortunately, even in the beginning stages, reading cards for yourself and others is a rewarding and enlightening experience.

Before you begin, read through this guide book and familiarize yourself with the cards in the deck. Take a few minutes to look at and touch each card. Then shuffle to get them out of order. Decide where and how you will keep your deck. Some people like to place their deck in a silk bag. Some like another special container. They are happy on your altar or any other sacred space in your home. These cards want to connect with you in order to be the best tool that they can be.

Before a reading, center yourself. A nice practice is to hold the cards to your heart for a moment. You will feel your connection and the cards will absorb your intention.

STEP 1

ASK A QUESTION.

How to phrase a question:

DO ask open-ended questions!

DON'T ask for specific dates, names, or outcomes.

Examples of questions that won't work:

Who am I going to marry?

Should I move to _______?

What should I do for work?

Instead, ask questions such as:

What do I need to focus on to make room for love to come into my life?

What is getting in the way of me moving forward?

What talents and skills should I focus on to bring in money?

STEP 2

SHUFFLE THE CARDS.

When you are ready to start the reading, shuffle the cards. If you are doing this reading for yourself, think of the question you've decided on.

If you are doing this for someone else, have them shuffle the cards. Ask them to think of a question. You will know when to stop the shuffle. The person who is shuffling may also hear an inner voice say: "Now" or "Stop" or "Here." Or they may just have a "Knowing" that it is time to stop.

STEP 3

LAY OUT THE CARDS.

Lay out your cards in the layout you have decided on. (The following section will have some sample layouts and ideas on creating your own.)

STEP 4

SCAN THE CARDS.

Take some time to scan the cards that have been chosen. Notice if any element is represented more than the others. Are most animals from the air realm? The sea? Are there other themes running through? Forest? Jungle? Urban?

This is also a time when you want to empty your mind of any preconceived ideas on what the cards "should" say. Let the images enter your subconscious. Let them speak to you. These cards will become an extension of your intuition with practice and usage.

STEP 5

READ THE CARDS.

Start with the first card in the layout and find the definition in this book. A card is designed to be read on its own and to also be read in conjunction with the cards surrounding it. This may seem daunting at first, but as you become familiar with the cards, their meanings, and the different layouts, this will become more and more effortless to you. This isn't a one-size-fits-all process. These cards are meant to facilitate a conversation—either with yourself and your guides or the person you are reading for. They will assist you in seeing the truth and energetically connecting to the animals that appear in your reading. Do not be surprised if after pulling a certain card, that animal starts to show themselves to you in other ways!

STEP 6

SUMMARIZE.

At the end of the reading, after going through the cards in the layout, you can summarize for yourself or the person you are reading for.

Find Your Animal Totem or Spirit Guide

The simplest way to make a path for your totem animal to make themselves known to you is to pull a card. I would suggest this only if you truly have no idea about what animal that might be. The reason is that this deck is not a comprehensive collection of all the possible animal spirit guides. But if you have no idea, and you were guided to this deck, then your guide is here.

Simply sit with the cards, after thoroughly shuffling. If you have previously used this deck to read for others (or even yourself) make an effort to cleanse the deck of all the older energies that may be lingering on it. You can use sage or palo-santo to smudge. You can use some quartz crystals (place one on top of the deck over night), put the deck on a windowsill during a full moon, or simply sleep with the deck under your pillow. (Wrap it in a scarf so as not to wake up to "44 pick up" all over your room the next morning!)

After you feel they have been thoroughly cleansed and shuffled, sit in a quiet meditative state for a few minutes. State your intention, either out loud, or in your mind's voice, and choose a card.

Alternately, you can choose three cards, and ask that among these three, for the universe to show you which animal is your guide. Over the next few days to two weeks, take note of what animal comes to you in different ways. Develop a relationship to that animal when they make themselves known to you. There is a saying that goes: "*If you do not sing and dance with your totem, they will leave you.*" Think about a friend who may ask for advice all the time. You give them advice, but they never take it. After a while, though you still love your friend, you stop giving them advice! Honor this relationship as sacred. If you have a home altar, find a representation of them to put up there or maybe a painting or photo that moves you.

Card Layouts

There are numerous layouts you can use for an oracle card reading. There is no right or wrong way to pull the cards. You can use as many or as few cards as you feel called to.

The Single-Card Layout

The single-card layout is a way to gain insight on a specific question, to receive daily guidance, or as an inquiry regarding the energy of the day. Simply shuffle the cards as directed and choose the first card on the top of the deck. Sometimes I add to the complexity by looking at the card at the bottom of the deck to determine the foundation of the question being asked (this can be done for all of the layouts).

The Three-Card Layout

This is another simple and fast layout. Traditionally, the cards are shuffled and placed from left to right. The far left card indicates the past, the middle card the present, and

the card on the right the future. You can actually assign any meaning to each card placement that you want.

The other meanings you can assign to a three-card spread are:

CARD 1	CARD 2	CARD 3
Situation You want	**Challenge** They want	**Guidance** Where the relationship is headed
Mind Present	**Body** 3 months	**Spirit** 6 months
Goal Situation	**Pros** Can Change	**Cons** Can't Change

THE FIVE-CARD LAYOUT

A five-card spread will give you a little more depth in the answers it offers. As in the spreads before, shuffle the cards and lay them out.

Card 1: Represents the relevant past.

Card 2: Represents the energy surrounding the situation right now.

Card 3: Indicates possible hidden issues affecting the situation.

Card 4: Indicates a possible action/advice to take for the highest possible outcome.

Card 5: Represents the most likely outcome if you follow the advice of the previous card.

Notes on Interpretations

There are a few things I would like to note about reading with *The Wild Elemental Oracle* deck. Unlike Tarot cards, there are no reversal meanings. These cards are a bit more straightforward. The clearer you are with your question, the clearer the cards will be. If, while shuffling, a card seems to "jump" out of the deck, take it and put it to the side. This is an indication that the energy in the card has a place in the reading, but more of a general place in the overall theme, rather than a specific meaning.

Buy a beautiful journal solely to use with your readings. After a while of writing down your readings, the date, the cards pulled, and the situation asked about, go back and look for themes. What animal keeps showing up? What element is predominant in your readings?

Many times, we are given what we need to know, not necessarily what we want to know. If you find yourself asking the same question over and over trying to get the answers you want. Stop. Put the cards away and go indulge in some self-care. When we are in a state of mind where the emotions are overriding our ability to take a step back, we are not able to be an open conduit for our guides to be heard. Take a walk, go see a friend, take a long bath . . . do something that grounds you, makes you happy, and takes your mind off whatever situation you are concerned with. When you have gotten to a place where you can objectively hear the advice you are seeking, try again.

ORACLE CARD MEANINGS

EARTH

1 WOLF

EARTH

WOLF ATTRIBUTES:

- Facing the end of a cycle with dignity and courage
- Death and rebirth
- Spirit teaching
- Guidance in dreams and meditations
- Instinct linked with intelligence
- Social and familial values
- Outwitting enemies
- Protection of self and family

When wolf appears, he is reminding you that you have a wild spirit even though you wear a cloak of civility. The wolf is a social creature, living within a pack that has a definite social hierarchy. There is always a balance between the members. The wolf is bringing you the message to find the balance between your own needs, your packs needs, and the needs of your community.

Also, pay attention to your dreams; your higher self is trying to get your attention.

2 BEAR

EARTH

BEAR ATTRIBUTES:

- Introspection
- Healing
- Solitude/Hibernation
- Spirit communication
- Death and rebirth
- Transformation
- Astral travel
- Creature of dreams, shamans and mystics
- Visionaries
- Defense and revenge
- Wisdom

Bear is telling you that it is time to go within and explore the reasons for your concern about this situation. Go deep into your heart and examine your journey and your path. Do you feel that this is the true path for you?

Going within sometimes means withdrawing from our normal group of friends for a time. Do not feel guilty if you are led to do this. You can only give to the people you care about if you are filled first.

3 BADGER

EARTH

BADGER ATTRIBUTES:

- Storyteller
- Aggressiveness
- Single-mindedness
- Passion
- Cunning
- Revenge
- Perseverance
- Groundedness
- Knowledge of the Earth
- Earth magic and wisdom

When Badger shows up in your life, you are being told that you have to own the right to walk your path at your own pace. Trust that you are exactly where you need to be and that all you need to walk this path is being given to you. Stay grounded in the present moment, and be confident that wherever you are, that is where you are supposed to be. Badgers create many burrows and typically roam from burrow to burrow, never staying at one for very long.

The aggressive nature of the Badger is giving you the message that you are well within your rights to get upset if someone is trespassing on your good will, your kind heart, or your path in life.

4 WORM
EARTH

WORM ATTRIBUTES:

- Regeneration
- Purifies the soil
- Ability to find nurturing within the Earth
- Camouflage
- Ability to wiggle out of difficult situations

When worm wiggles into your life, he brings the message not to worry about a difficult situation. Access your deep intuition and follow your instincts. Spend time outside, and give over your worries and troubles to the earth. Practice grounding outside with bare feet. It will work wonders on clearing clouds of worry from your mind.

5 STAG

EARTH

STAG ATTRIBUTES:

- Gentleness
- Ability to move through life with grace
- Innocence
- Sensitivity
- Intuition
- Ability to change directions quickly

The stag shows up in your life when you need to quiet the inner critic and be gentle with yourself. Give to yourself the understanding and kindness that you are wont to give others. None of us are perfect. We are all on this road to learn and grow. Growth does not happen without walking a challenging path, and with that comes making mistakes. If you are not making mistakes, you are not growing!

When it comes to your relationships with others, know that you cannot force change on anyone. All you can do is gently show them a new path by walking it yourself.

6 Bison (Buffalo)

EARTH

BISON (BUFFALO) ATTRIBUTES:

- Feminine courage
- Abundance
- Knowledge
- Generosity
- Hospitality
- Sharing work
- Courage
- Strength
- Challenge
- Survival
- Giving for the greater good

The native tribes in the plains of the United States revered the buffalo as sacred. This animal fed, clothed, and created tools and medicine for the tribe. The people honored the buffalo for its sacrifice for the good of the tribe. Every bit of the animal was used. To waste any part would be an affront to the sacrifice the animal made.

You are being shown that abundance is all around you. You will always have everything you need. Keep yourself in the energy of gratitude, and honor every aspect of your life. Be grateful for everything you have and you will stay in the sacred energy of gratitude and abundance.

Alternatively, this totem could also be reminding you that you need to stay grounded as you work toward greater abundance. Your path toward success is equally as important as the goals that you accomplish.

7 ANT
EARTH

ANT ATTRIBUTES:

- Patience
- Stamina
- Planning
- The energy and patience needed to complete work
- Communal living
- Storing for the future

When ant comes into your life, he is showing you how to join forces and work for the common good. The whole is stronger than the sum of their parts, as the saying goes. If you are struggling with an issue, definitely look outside yourself to get help in solving the problem.

Put your head down, gather up all of your resources, have patience, and know that your continued, diligent effort will show results.

8 RABBIT

EARTH

RABBIT ATTRIBUTES:

- Living by your wits
- Receiving hidden teachings and intuitive messages
- Quick-thinking
- Humility
- Moving through fear
- Strengthening intuition
- Fertility

Rabbit tells you that you have everything you need, though some of your skills and gifts may need to be developed further. You have an idea of what you want to do and where you want to go. Move through the fear that is keeping you from moving forward. Your creativity is high right now, take advantage of it. Look out for a possible windfall of abundance (and all aspects that abundance covers) is imminent.

9 SNAKE
EARTH

SNAKE ATTRIBUTES:

- Elusiveness
- Transmutation
- Exploration of the mysteries of life
- Elemental energy
- Goddess energy
- Psychic energy
- Creative power
- Immortality

Snake slithering across your path is letting you know that transformation is now in progress. In other words, you will be shedding old skin and emotions and transforming them into something bigger and better. There is no need to fear the changes that are happening. This is on your path and snake is asking you to have clear in your mind and heart your intention for this transformation.

10 GIRAFFE

EARTH

GIRAFFE ATTRIBUTES:

- Sees far into the future
- Ability to reach things that are unreachable to others
- Communication
- Intuition
- Ability to remain above chaos

Giraffe points out that deep in your heart, you knew some of this already. Your intuition and foresight: even though you may not been able to explain why you knew this, you did. Listen to your gut.

You are also being asked to search your heart and gut, or your discernment, to see how things "feel" to you. If it feels good, move forward. If something feels off, search to see if there is a hidden fear; if there is, look to healing that fear. If not, listen to that small voice telling you to look at another direction.

11 MOLE

EARTH

MOLE ATTRIBUTES:

- Guardian of the lower regions
- Connection with Earth energies
- Knowledge of herbs, roots, minerals, elements, and plant medicine
- Ability to turn inward
- Introspection
- Love expressed in nature
- Sensitivity to touch and vibration
- Understanding of energies

Mole popping up in your life is a sign to look inward for your special connection to the Earth and all the energies inherent around you. You can find your answers in your ability to go within and focus on what the energy of a situation is telling you. Take your time; when you are in the dark about a situation, do not rush or assume. Slowly and quietly gather the facts, and listen to the energies and what they are trying to tell you. Do not let anyone else sway you; burrow down and stay your course. You will arrive at the decision you were meant to.

ORACLE CARD MEANINGS

WATER

12 DOLPHIN

WATER

DOLPHIN ATTRIBUTES:

- Importance of play
- Change
- Wisdom
- Balance
- Harmony
- Communication skills
- Freedom
- Trust

Dolphin shows up to remind you to get out with your friends and family and play. Take a break from being an adult with all of its inherent responsibilities and seriousness. Play! This will bring the emotions of joy, fun, happiness, movement, and freedom into your life. Playing will add a new dimension to your relationships. You are being led to get more in touch with the childlike, playful side of yourself.

13 WHALE

WATER

WHALE ATTRIBUTES:

- Akashic Records
- Power of voice
- Psychic and telepathic abilities
- All aspects of the sea
- Beauty of movement

When whale swims into your life, you are being reminded that your life is yours to live. You are prompted to follow your heart's song. What makes you unique is a key to what you are here to do. Do not try to make yourself a weak copy of someone else or what others want you to be. Sing your song and sing it proud!

Alternately, you are being reassured that while you cannot know everything, you can be assured that all you have to do is trust and have faith that what your heart desires will come to you in the right time and in the right way.

14 SEAL

WATER

SEAL ATTRIBUTES:

- Protection during change
- Lucid dreaming
- Protection from danger
- Movement through emotions
- Creativity

When seal slides into your life, you are being told that this is the time to pay close attention to your hunches, your dreams, even your daydreams; they are all working to manifest your reality in an extra strong way right now. Take advantage of this time and dream big! The sky is the limit.

15 TURTLE
WATER

TURTLE ATTRIBUTES:

- Symbol of the Earth
- Connection with the center
- Navigation skills
- Patience
- Self-boundaries
- Feminine energy
- Psychically protecting oneself
- Self-reliance
- Non-violent defense

Turtle crawls into your life with the message that "slow and steady wins the race." Do not feel that you have to force or push a situation. Nor should you take shortcuts or skip steps. Take your time; let everything unfold at the right time. Relax and trust in the process.

Alternately she is telling you that this situation will unfold in a slow and steady manner. Do not rush it. Stay grounded and enjoy the process.

16 KOI

WATER

KOI ATTRIBUTES:

- Prosperity
- Beauty
- Harmony
- Balance between mind and emotion
- Peace

When you see Koi swimming into your life, expect abundance—not only of money, but also of resources, luck, love, friendship, opportunities, and creativity!

This is a time to take advantage of all that you are being offered and have access to. This is an ideal time to work on a transformation you have been dreaming about.

17 STARFISH

WATER

STARFISH ATTRIBUTES:

- Regeneration
- Moon magic
- Beauty
- Connection to the star people
- Tidal movement

Finding Starfish on your path is a message and lesson to let go of things that no longer serve you. When you can easily and gracefully let go of what you no longer need, you open the door for what *will* serve you to come in.

Work with the moon cycle: the new moon to let go and the full moon to invite. This is a powerful way to attune you to the rhythms of life. The ebb and flow of letting go and bringing in is right, timely, and powerful.

18 SPIDER

WATER

SPIDER ATTRIBUTES:

- Weaver of the web of fate
- Wisdom
- Creativity
- Divine inspiration
- Shapeshifting
- Understanding the patterns of illusion
- Female energy for the creative force of life

When Spider weaves her way into your life, she brings with her some powerful messages. A master creator, she is encouraging you to express yourself in a creative form. Beyond that, she is showing you that we are all the creators of our own lives. Only you have the power to weave the life you want. Stop waiting for something to happen to you; create what you want to happen!

Stop ignoring your ideas and dreams; reach in, grab your creativity, and start putting it to use. Creativity is not solely regulated to the arts. Problem solving is creative. Business is creative. Relationships thrive when injected with a big dose of creativity!

19 FROG

WATER

FROG ATTRIBUTES:

- Singer of songs
- Transformation
- Cleansing
- Understanding emotions
- Rebirth

When frog hops into your life, you are being nudged to actively look for opportunities for transitions. You may be facing some of life's tough challenges, and Frog messages and lessons will help you swim through these changes with grace and ease. The awakening that accompanies these changes will bring greater abundance into your life.

Alternatively, frog medicine is also symbolic of coming into your power. This is done by purifying the soul, releasing emotional baggage, and coming from a place of personal integrity. Frog is telling you to make all your choices based on what is best for you.

20 JELLYFISH

WATER

JELLYFISH ATTRIBUTES:

- Sensitivity to emotions
- Understanding of the value of floating, rather than swimming, through trying emotional times
- Proper use of softness (not being rigid)
- Ability to become untangled from the webs of peril in life

Jellyfish shows you that you can shine the brightest by just being yourself. By living a very transparent life you will be brought to the epitome of authenticity. Do not be afraid of letting others see you for who you really are. Your strength lies in your ability to be vulnerable. Go with the flow and allow yourself to feel the emotions and react to what is being presented to you at any particular time. Let go of the rigidity of thinking.

21 SALMON

WATER

SALMON ATTRIBUTES:

- Value of returning home
- Successfully swimming upstream through the emotional
- Understanding divine messages
- Rebirth of spiritual knowledge

When you see Salmon swimming into your life, you are being shown that the struggle you are facing may seem insurmountable, but just know that the most resistance is just before you succeed. Do not give up. Put all your faith, power, passion, and energy into achieving what it is you are working toward!

Going against the current, while exhausting at times, also brings you the experience of a journey that forced you to give it your all and the pride of a huge accomplishment. Make sure that you are able to detach yourself from the emotions that maybe weighing you down.

22 GULL
WATER

GULL ATTRIBUTES:

- Spiritual messengers
- Communication with spirits
- Behaving responsibly
- Ability to see from above
- Friendship

When you have Gull soaring into your life, you are being asked to look at this situation from a different perspective. Take a step back, detach from any expectations you have, and look with new eyes. See if there are any hidden tools or resources that you couldn't see before. Shift your attitude the way a gull shifts on the current and you will get to where you need to go.

ORACLE CARD MEANINGS

FIRE

23 HUMMINGBIRD

FIRE

HUMMINGBIRD ATTRIBUTES:

- Ability to heal by using light
- Endurance over long journeys
- Ability to fly into small places to heal
- Joy
- Happiness
- Love

When Hummingbird is darting into your life, he is bringing the message to bring more joy into your life. Even though you may be caught up in the drama and the chaos that is surrounding you, make time to get away from all of it and play. You can find the time to do the things that make you happy. Try not to bring your worries into these play dates with yourself.

You can believe that the end to the drama is right around the corner. You have a hand in manifesting your own happiness, love, and joy. Move forward onto this path!

24 TIGER

FIRE

TIGER ATTRIBUTES:

- Power
- Energy
- Strength and willpower
- Acting in a timely manner

When Tiger prowls into your reading, this is a reminder that persistence is what is necessary in order to attain your goals. Be patient; do not over think things, this will lead to paralysis. Tap into your determination and will to get there. You will succeed—but only through patience.

Alternatively this big cat may be telling you that careful planning is needed. Even if what you need to do is not at the top of your list of favorite things, keep plugging away and know that you can and will get this done!

25 LION

FIRE

LION ATTRIBUTES:

- Brotherhood
- Letting go of stress
- Strong family ties
- Strength
- Courage
- Energy
- Self-fulfillment

The majestic Lion appears when leadership is needed. The true leader is one who supports those around him, has patience, and uses empathy, compassion, and wisdom to get the work done! Stay away from bossy and dictator behavior; this will not get you what you desire. Look to bring balance into your life and this situation. Take time to not only work, but to relax and de-stress.

26 SALAMANDER

FIRE

SALAMANDER ATTRIBUTES:

- Transformation
- Soul memories
- Change
- Comfort in darkness
- Ability to cloak in the face of adversity

Change is what Salamander brings to your situation. But he is asking you to be a proactive participant with this change. Use your time wisely; reach back into the memory of your earlier times, and pull forth the lessons that were presented back then. Have you learned from them? Or are you repeating the same lessons over and over? If so, make conscious changes to move yourself forward and put that lesson to bed once and for all.

27 BEE
FIRE

BEE ATTRIBUTES:

- Hard work
- Social
- Female warrior energy
- Reincarnation
- Communication with the dead
- Concentration
- Prosperity

Bee comes buzzing into your life when you need to watch how you are being productive. Are you getting lost in an inability to be orderly and efficient? Are you missing opportunities due to disorganization? Are you missing working with others to achieve your goals?

What are your goals? How can you get there? Step by step, write down what it will take for you to get there. What gets in your way of achieving these steps?

28 DRAGON

FIRE

DRAGON ATTRIBUTES:

- Born of Fire
- Protector
- Exists between thoughts
- Ability to move between worlds
- Connection to the birth of the Universe

A very powerful messenger, the Dragon appears when major life changes are happening or about to happen. He is with you as a reminder that you have the power to get through these changes! You are being shown that though these changes or situation may seem overwhelming and life-altering, it is a catalyst for major spiritual growth. It is not often that this amount of power enters your life at the same time as transformational changes. Harness and make the most of it!

29 PHOENIX
FIRE

PHOENIX ATTRIBUTES:

- Rising from the ashes
- Death and Rebirth
- Keeper of the fire of creation
- Transformation
- Walking boldly on a difficult path

A mythical figure, the phoenix is able to burn and regenerate from its ashes. Not a gentle process, this is an act that always leads to a transformation.

Do not be afraid. If Phoenix has come into your life, allow what is happening to unfold. Know that you are strong enough to stand in this fire and come out the other side transformed.

30 LADY BUG

FIRE

LADYBUG ATTRIBUTES:

- Good luck
- Past lives
- Spiritual enlightenment
- Death and Rebirth

Ladybug appearing in your life heralds a time of luck—when the seeds that you have planted will start to unfurl and you will see the results of your hard work.

Sometimes this good luck comes after a time of darkness; know that this happened for a reason, and going forward joy and happiness will start to push out the darkness.

31 SCORPION

FIRE

SCORPION ATTRIBUTES:

- Attacking from the rear
- Death and rebirth
- Transmutation of poison
- Reflecting dark and negative energy back to its sender

Scorpion may not be the warm fuzzy you want to see in your life, but it shows up when cutting something or someone out of your life is timely and necessary.

When we work on ourselves to heal and move forward on our spiritual path, we start to see wondrous changes, but with this growth, we also see people, situations, and things falling away from our lives. This is always needed. It may not feel like it is. When scorpion shows up, trust that it is ultimately for your highest best.

32 COUGAR

FIRE

COUGAR ATTRIBUTES:

- The proper use of leadership and power
- Balancing power, intention, strength, and grace
- Self-confidence
- Freedom from guilt
- Sensuality
- Cunning
- Enigma

A solitary cat, when you catch Cougar prowling into your life, he is bringing to you the message that you have come into your own power. Now is the time to take the lead in a situation. Now is the time to be strong. He is here to let you know that now is the time to leap into all the opportunities made available to you. Using the power of intentions, be clear with your purpose and define where you are heading.

33 COBRA

FIRE

COBRA ATTRIBUTES:

- Soul guide
- Moving quickly
- Memory of the soul world
- Transmutation of the soul
- Past-life memories
- Wisdom of the Goddess

Cobra poking his head into your life is showing you that soon unexpected opportunities will be showing themselves, and you must be prepared to strike quickly. Do not pay too much attention to what others will say about this. Hone in on your intuition and move swiftly and decisively!

Alternately, are you stuck in a seemingly impossible-to-break fixation on something or someone? Snap out of it! This is preventing you from taking advantage of all of the promising opportunities that are around you; you need to see them!

ORACLE CARD MEANINGS

AIR

34 BAT

AIR

BAT ATTRIBUTES:

- Shamanic death and rebirth
- Initiation
- Viewing past lives
- Understanding grief
- Use of vibrational sound
- Camouflage
- Invisibility
- Ability to observe unseen

When Bat silently appears into your life, she is putting you on notice that major changes are heading your way. Pay attention to the subtle things that will herald these changes. These could be emotional, spiritual, physical, or material.

This change will pertain to the death of a part of you that no longer serves the you that you are becoming. You have the choice of embracing these changes or fighting them. Be aware that they *will* happen, and it will be much easier on you if you embrace them. You are becoming the highest version of yourself!

35 BUTTERFLY

AIR

BUTTERFLY ATTRIBUTES:

- Reincarnation
- Transformation
- Transmutation
- Magic

When Butterfly floats into your life, you are being asked to accept the transformation you are in the middle of. The physical reaction to the energetic changes may be alarming at first. You are being reminded that everything is energy and the acceptance of that allows you to gracefully slip through this transformation with grace and ease. See this as a wondrous validation that magic is real and alive in your life. Celebrate this by dancing, singing, and just loving the physical experience that living in out bodies provides us!

Alternatively, butterfly can bring us the message that we are all on a long journey of the soul. During this adventure, there will be constant turns, changes, shifts, and dips that will cause us to respond and change. That is the beauty of living in the moment and not holding on to ties to the past. We are free to change as circumstances demand.

36 EAGLE

AIR

EAGLE ATTRIBUTES:

- Swiftness
- Strength
- Keen sight
- Illumination of Spirit
- Creation
- Ability to see hidden spiritual truths
- Connection to spirit guides and teachers
- Great power and balance
- Dignity with grace
- Connection with higher truths
- Intuitive and creative spirit

When Eagle soars into you life, it is never quiet or subtle. Eagle is a sign to reconnect with your spiritual path. She is showing you the way to the highest of your personal truth. The guidance she brings is one of the heart and your higher self. The sky is the limit when you follow your highest directives.

What is it that your heart desires? How does this tie in with your spiritual path? What is the bigger picture of these two things combined? As long as you are open, listen and allow; eagle will show you the way.

37 HAWK

AIR

HAWK ATTRIBUTES:

- Clear-sightedness
- Being observant
- Messages from spirit
- Guardianship
- Recalling past lives
- Illumination
- Seeing the larger picture
- Creativity
- Truth
- Experience
- Wise use of opportunities
- Overcoming problems

Hawk is a message and points to omens. Pay attention; spirit will be giving you some messages. Ordinary life is never quite that ordinary. Signs and symbols are all around you. Watch, listen, and be still so you can hear what is being said. What is holding you back from soaring to the greatest heights?

38 OWL

AIR

OWL ATTRIBUTES:

- Stealth
- Secrecy
- Silent and swift movement
- Seeing behind masks
- Keen sight
- Messenger of secrets and omens
- Shape-shifting
- Link between the dark, unseen world and the world of light
- Comfort with shadow self
- Moon magic
- Freedom

Owl comes to you when she needs you to see things that are being hidden from you. Pay attention; secrets are about to be revealed. Be proactive and allow yourself to accept the information. Do not react, but when you choose to act, come from a place of wisdom and clear sight. Know that not all is as it seems.

39 FOX

AIR

FOX ATTRIBUTES:

- Shape shifting
- Cleverness
- Observational skills
- Cunning
- Stealth
- Camouflage
- Feminine courage
- Invisibility
- Ability to observe unseen
- Persistence
- Gentleness
- Swiftness

When Fox bounds into your life, she is showing you that you have the ability to solve any problem. Use all of your skills to find the answer. She can lead you to a new way of seeing the solution. Have patience and do not rush the answer, but stay quiet until you are sure you can solve the problem. Gather all the information you need. You will see the issue for what it really is, to see behind the masks and illusion.

40 FLAMINGO

AIR

FLAMINGO ATTRIBUTES:

- Ability to filter soul lessons from emotional waters
- Understanding the language of color
- Ability to maintain soul purpose in group living
- Understanding how to maintain balance

Flamingo makes an appearance in your life when you need to hear that no matter what is going on in your life, even if it's a drama-filled situation, there is always a take-away lesson. She is here to show you that nothing happens that is not suppose to. Finding the lesson is critical to be able to staying away from the lower vibration emotions that you are experiencing.

Take out a piece of paper and list possible lessons. You may not be in a place to see them right now, so use your imagination. Stuck in traffic and going to be late? Perhaps if you were on time, you would be in an accident. Once you start training yourself to look at situations in this way, life becomes very much less frustrating!

41 PRAYING MANTIS

AIR

PRAYING MANTIS ATTRIBUTES:

- Ability to manipulate time
- Power to move between moments
- Understanding of the circular nature of time
- Power of stillness
- Female warrior energy
- Attack strategy

Usually the Praying Mantis makes an appearance when we've flooded our lives with so much business, activity, or chaos that we can no longer hear the still, small voice within us. Taking a step back and some simple meditation would be in order here, because the external din we've created needs to be quieted so that we can come back to our own truth. She will always come to us when we need peace, quiet, and calm in our lives.

42 HERON

AIR

HERON ATTRIBUTES:

- Independence
- Self-reliance
- Boundaries
- Exploration
- Self-esteem
- Balancing multiple tasks
- Dignity

Heron is all about independence and all of its trappings. When Heron arrives with messages, she is letting you know that you got this! In order for you to soar to the heights that you were born to, take care that you also stay grounded. Only then will you be able to reach your potential.

Find your boundaries; do not let others take advantage of you. When you start to *wiffle-waffle* with others, take it as an opportunity to look deep into what about you is unwilling to keep healthy boundaries. Heron brings lessons that can be challenging, but on the other side is a freedom and peace that is priceless!

43 ROADRUNNER

AIR

ROADRUNNER ATTRIBUTES:

- Proper use of speed
- Understanding rapid change
- Agility
- Evading capture through quickness

Just like the cartoon from years ago, which pitted a certain coyote against his nemesis, the roadrunner bursts into your life to put you on notice that you will need to make some quick decisions in the near future! There are ideas that you have percolated, possibly waiting for the exact right time to implement . . . well, that time is here and now. Stop waiting; trust that you have everything you need to move forward with your ideas and plans. Muster up all the motivation you need, break it down into small steps, and then . . . GO!

Alternately, like our cartoon buddy, this may be a warning that there maybe roadblocks ahead. But know that by being present, aware, and trusting in your capabilities you will be able to think on your feet and turn these roadblocks to your advantage.

44 PEACOCK
AIR

PEACOCK ATTRIBUTES:

- All aspects of beauty
- Immortality
- Ability to see into the past, present, and future
- Dignity
- Self-confidence

Peacock/hen struts into your life to let you know that nothing in this life is permanent. Our soul is the only immortal thing we possess. Stop taking things so seriously! Lighten up! Let go of preconceived notions on how this all has to turn out. Play, laugh, and let go. This is the best medicine we have. Have the confidence that what is yours is yours. What is not yours, no matter the manipulations or energy you put out trying to get or keep, ultimately will not last. Have the dignity and self confidence to let what will be, be.

DELVE INTO THE WORLD
OF ANIMALS AND YOU WILL
CONNECT WITH THE
PRIMAL CORE OF WHO
YOU REALLY ARE...AND WHO
YOU ARE MEANT TO BE.

—MICHELLE MOTUZUS

CONCLUSION

I hope you can see that there is a world of information, lessons, wisdom, and messages that we can glean from the animal kingdom. I hope this deck inspires and encourages a deeper relationship with the animals around you.

Trust your gut and stay open to the guides that you will meet on the glorious path of self-discovery and empowerment that you are on!

NOTES

WHEN YOU ALLOW

THE ANIMAL KINGDOM

INTO YOUR LIFE, YOU WILL

HEAR THE SECRETS THAT

WILL MAKE UP ALL

THE WISDOM IN THE WORLD.

—MICHELLE MOTUZUS

ABOUT THE AUTHOR / ARTIST

Native New Englander **Michelle A. Motuzas** started painting in answer to the requests of her fellow students of Shamanism, which led to the drawings that are used in her first deck, *The Shamanic Healing Oracle Cards*. In her art, nature mirrors the human condition. Exploring our spiritual and human existence within the bounds of natural imagery, and drawing on her background in Shamanistic studies, Michelle learned the importance of symbolism in the human psyche. The root of these symbols helps her identify what she wants to create with her art, a connection between the energy of the physical and spiritual being.

The proud mother of two boys, Michelle also has her masters in Shamanic Reiki and is a certified healer and medium.

FIND OUT MORE INFORMATION ABOUT MICHELLE AT

WWW.MICHELLEAMOTUZAS.COM

SHAMANIC HEALING ORACLE CARDS

MICHELLE A. MOTUZAS

Explore your spiritual and human existence within the bounds of natural imagery.

Look into the energies, fears, and wrong beliefs that are holding you back from having the best life possible. Via Shamanism studies, these 44 beautifully drawn oracle cards on black background will help you learn the importance of symbolism in the human psyche. Discover for yourself and others the energies surrounding situations in life that can hinder or assist you along your path of self-awareness and healing. Whether a novice or skilled reader, the messages found in these cards and the accompanying guidebook will give you the insight, personal empowerment, and trust in your own intuitive abilities and will allow you to begin an energetic healing journey that is precisely tailored to you. Consider the universal symbols and energetic messages these cards have for you. Begin living a life of spiritual clarity, energetic oneness, and personal empowerment.

Box set: 3½" × 5" × 1½"
44 art cards | 120 pp
ISBN: 978-0-7643-5036-8
$24.99

INTUITIVE WISDOM

COLOR-YOUR-DECK TAROT CARDS

MICHELLE A. MOTUZAS

This innovative Tarot deck taps into your creativity, intuition, and inner guidance to create a personally colored deck.

Resonates with you on a deep, intimate soul level but also allows you to become your own best oracle! Create your own imaginative Tarot project that invites greater access to your intuition and wisdom of the higher self, empowering you to find your path to healing and wholeness. Using the meditative and artistic action of coloring, harness your awareness and receive messages that the Tarot offers by coloring 78 artcards showing animal archetypes. Immerse yourself into the primal lessons from the animal kingdom and infuse the cards with your own beautiful and unique energy as you explore this tool for your spiritual journey. Includes 78 Tarot cards to color, informative guidebook, and colored pencils.

Box set: 6" × 9" × 2"
78 art cards | 96 pp
ISBN: 978-0-7643-6020-6
$34.99

LIFE IS MAGICAL . . .

WHEN YOU ALLOW IT TO BE.

—MICHELLE MOTUZUS